POTTY MOUTH, POTTY MOUTH

ALEX CREECE

POTTY MOUTH

ALEX CREECE

POTTY MOUTH

BOOK 08

SERIES 5

CORDITE BOOKS

First printed in 2024
by Cordite Publishing Inc.

PO Box 58
Castlemaine 3450
Victoria, Australia
cordite.org.au | korditebooks.org.au

National Library of Australia
Cataloguing-in-Publication:

Creece, Alex
Po y Mouth, Po y Mouth
978-0-6457616-1-0 paperback
I. Title.
A821.3

Poetry set in Rabenau 10 / 15
Cover design by Zoë Sadokierski
Text design by Kent MacCarter and Zoë Sadokierski
Printed and bound by McPhersons in Maryborough, Victoria

 is collection was wri en on the stolen Wadawurrung and Woiwurrung lands of the Kulin Nation. Storytelling has existed here for thousands of years, and we pay our respects and to the traditional custodians of the lands, skies, waterways on which we live, work and rest. Always was, always will be.

10 9 8 7 6 5 4 3 2 1

For Munawar Sarker (1994–2018)
I never sent my last le   er.
I hope you get this one.

For Ziggy (2011–2023)
You are my heart.
It's shaped like a hippo, and it smells like corn chips.

To those whose stumbling feet begin at the tip of
the tongue, Sing, Daddy, Sing.

Collage poem from *Irving's Anatomy Mnemonics*

CONTENTS

PREFACE

is book is a testament to the idea that if you keep writing, something will form. Some of those shapes will be emojis, goop stains, paper cuts and everyday geometries. Trash and art are incestuous lovers, and I'm hoarding their o spring.

I'm an ugly talker, screeching like a pissbaby. I know that this book could be described as confessional – a gendered accusation, and a dirty word when trying to evade the constraints of both gender and genre. I've never read a poem that didn't confess anything, didn't betray the heart of its author. And I've never read a cringe-free poem, nor do I want to.

I was once deemed a basket case, and now that basket is filled with astro flu , orbited by spinning tornado cows. Now my basket is hitched to a unicycle, discarded at the clown orgy. Now my basket is empty again.

I'm a naïve artist and a foolish poet. I eat MILF cereal and I have no money. I don't know how to talk to anyone, much less an imagined reader. I cut and scissor in equal measures, and I encourage you to tear this book apart if you see fit.

I hope you fall into something sticky within these pages, or lose your keys, or your marbles.

You are wonderful. Taste my spit.

INTRODUCTION

Alex Creece's *Potty Mouth, Potty Mouth* is a reckless, glorious, gro y revolution. It's an insubordinate 'kissyface of cobwebs' that sticks it to capitalism, heteronormativity and the patriarchy.

e poems tap into our senses: the reader *sees* the visual cyber '0NLY 5CR34M'; *hears* the 'amphibian alchemy' of 'galumphs' and 'la-di-da-di-das'; *smells* public transport's cocktail of cologne 'fighting for atmospheric dominance'; *tastes* the dirt gnawed o garden gloves, the 'sick ickness' of dry-retching, the hocked phlegm and chew of a spit ball; and *feels* the etch of 'friction-burnt knees' and 'pores scrubbed raw but never unfilthy'.

One thing this text doesn't – rightfully – shy away from is queerness. rough 'high glitching lavender lechery', Creece proves to be the death of the wholesome ingénue, and is defiantly not 'the kind of gay that fits comfortably within a Kmart catalogue.' ese poems subvert traditional tales of womanhood via dyke culture by 'reliving the gnaRled guts of a girlhood' and confessing to us, 'My coming out story is the ballad of Earring Magic Ken.'

Quotably horny and delightfully vulgar, *Potty Mouth, Potty Mouth* reeks of dirty talk via stream of consciousness slide-worthy DMs. e poem 'God Wants You to Come!' is a mash-up collage from pornography and religious magazines, which implores, 'BE BAPTISED. FAPWORTHY for the Lord.' While ' e Last 37.5mg' asks 'what if I le the vibrator gently buzzing in my nightstand / hornet's nest of horniness.'

Creece's words surge with anti-capitalist, anti-authoritarian sentiments: 'I pick my wedgie as I pass the fanciest mansion.' e poem 'Acne' describes the cologne-stenched rich folks waiting for the author's death so they 'can build a McMansion from my body', while zits are purported to be 'a bubble of billionaires oozing from the craters in my face.' Pimples are also seen as defiance and aliveness – 'Acne is when I let myself live', Creece writes. 'I just want skin. Bad skin. And I want for that to be okay.'

is book tells us it's okay to simultaneously desire deviance and defiance, while also wanting to retreat between the lines of poems. In psych wards full of 'the brain zapz and psyche scraps' where it's 'your duty to have fun', Creece asks us, 'how do I grow here?' Especially when, in the inescapable shadow of the a ermath of rape, 'I know now I was never / deranged, / only degraded to the point where I cannot / metabolise my own history.'

Potty Mouth, Potty Mouth examines the watchfulness and freedom of dirt, earth and garden, through the lens of a climate change conscious narrator who proclaims, 'I want to plant enough trees to o set my existence.' While in 'Mindblind', we are o ered the haunting image of 'a Milo tin / in the apocalypse. / Comforting, but for whom?'

It's a dirty, dykey, 90s-nostalgic text that, through existential and self-referential lines, asks us to question our inner grimy gremlin.   is work is a 'po y-mouth shitfaced double-knot' of a book from the 'cuntrarian gullet', and I am glad these poems never washed their mouths out with soap.

—Rae White

PERCEIVE

S C R E E C H   a er Benjamin Frater, the Catholic Yak

Pus
hing
the w
ords ‘oh
well’ as a
bruise int
o my skin g
li er in my t
ears (tears in m
y gli er) and sung
lasses on a midnigh
t train when the bar g
allops with B A D F E E
L I N G T H I S I S B A D
screaming over the Lizzie McGu
ire theme song as if Dr Seuss were
some kind of disgruntled lesbian shat
tered on the B A D B A D F E E L I N G
ferment this zeitgeist sticky stricken unst
uck cobwebs of cellulite I love you into a can
yon grande like frapuccino fates faded on the f
ri resign my blood-clo ed furies when a soul dr
ain clogs po y-mouth shitfaced double-knot the bra
instem and call it an experience for every fair-weather
ed dead-end frostbi en on the way to bed death and bon
e blisters and bubble o bill oh but always B A D F E E
L
I
N
G

Illusio

stuck in tenth grade bubblegum
fingernails and pencils
sharpened nouns that punctuate
the latest puncture
scraping across bubbled plastic le   over
lunchtimes I tripped
over myself on the texture
of the sun swampy
knee-pit years made you
sick from kedgeree and blaspheme
and if you are my refrigerator
mother, I spilled the milk

CH3353 5W34T5

EV4P0R4TE 01110110 01100001 01110000 01101111 01110010 01100001 01110100 01100101 00001010 01100001 4 DR34M 00100000 01100100 01110010 01100101 01100001 01101101 00001010 01101001 01101110 01110100 INT0 M1LK-F1LM L1P5 01101111 00100000 01101101 01101001 01101100 01101011 00101101 01100110 01101001 01101100 SL0BB3R3D C4T4R4CT5 01101101 00100000 01101100 01101001 01110000 01110011 00101110 00001010 01010011 01101100 C4T-3Y3D 01101111 01100010 01100010 01100101 01110010 01100101 00100000 01100011 4ND C0M4T053 01100001 01110100 01100001 01110010 01100001 01100011 01110100 T34CH M3 01110011 00111010 00001010 01100011 01100001 TH3 L4NGU4G3 0F 4 L05T G35TUR3 01110100 00101101 01100101 HUNG0V3R FR0M 5TR33TL1GHT5 01111001 01100101 01100100 00101100 00100000 01100011 01101111 01101101 01100001 01110100 4ND 50C14L 5PL4TT3R 01101111 01110011 01100101 00101110 00001010 01010100 01100101 01100001 01100011 01101000 F41L 00100000 01101101 01100101 00100000 01110100 01101000 01100101 00100000 01101100 01100001 TH3 F1R5T P4NC4K3 01101110 01100111 01110101 01100001 01100111 01100101 00100000 W1TH 01101111 01100110 00100000 01100001 01101100 01101111 D0UBL3-T4LK 01110011 01110100 00100000 01100111 01100101 01110011 T00 0N3-D1M3N510N4L 01110100 01110101 01110010 01100101 00101100 R3GURG1T4TE 00001010 01101000 01110101 01101110 01100111 01101111 01110110 TH3 B1L3 01100101 01110010 00100000 01100110 01110010 01101111 01101101 00100000 01110011 01110100 0F 4 L1F3 01110010 01100101 01100101 01110100 01101100 01101001 01100111 01101000 01110100 01110011 W0RTH L1V1NG 00100000 00001010 01100001 01101110 01100100 00100000 01110011 01101111 01100011 01101001 4ND 45K M3 01100001 01101100 00100000 01110011 01110000 01101100 01100001 01110100 01110100 01100101 WHY 01110010 00101110 00001010 01000110 01100001 01101001 01101100 00100000 01110100 01101000 1 C4NN0T WH15P3R 01100101 00100000 01100110 01101001 01110010 01110011 01110100 00100000 01110000 01100001 011011 0NLY 5CR34M

Dirty Talk

I know I'm low on iron
when I crave the dirts. I mix minerals,
supplements into my orange juice,
because vitamin Smut helps you absorb iron more e ectively,
did you know? And then the cravings subside.
But the supplements are expensive, so, sometimes
I live in a state of side-eyeing the dirts,
like it's a woman whose boyfriend is all earwax and static fuzz.
(I'm happy for them, of course,
of course.) I flirt with the dirts,
I think. At the kitchen sink, I gnaw
dirt o   the garden gloves. Friends
take supermarket selfies with
especially mud-caked potatoes,
later shopli   ed. I drool like a dancing bear.
Worse in winter,
when I'm bleeding constantly
and hungry for the warmth of gentle rain
on sleeping minerals.
My dog snu   es around in the backyard,
a slobbery sealion pretend-playing as a tru   e pig.
Her mind is an underground blueprint
of latitude tutus across every goat
horn and chew toy hidden. She walks back
through the dog door with a tell-tale mud-snout,
sneezing up secrets. I envy the trail of her whiskers
paving alleyways for ants
through a miniature wilderness.
I listen to 'Another One Bites the Dust',
and I wish I would, but literally.
Just let me fucking eat the dirts.

Shitpost collage from text messages

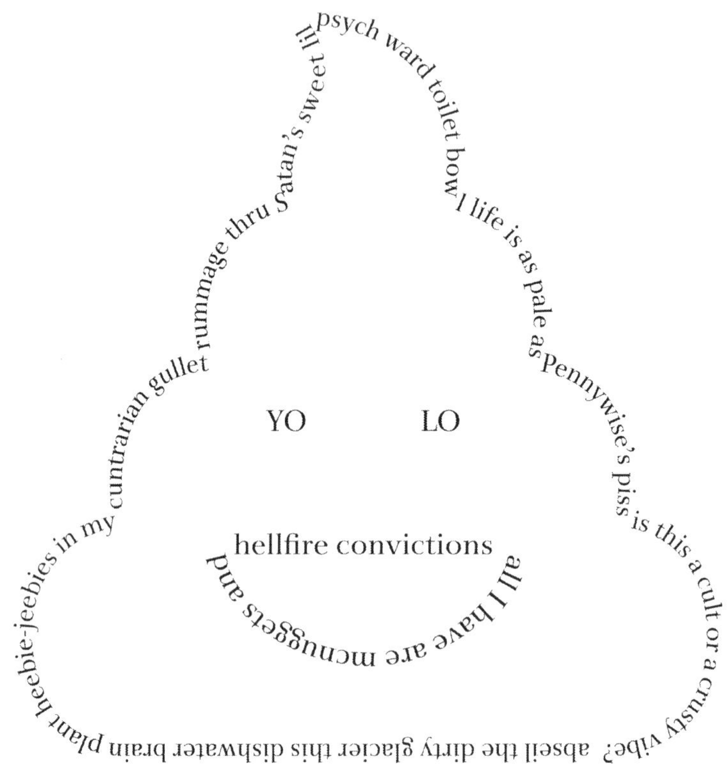

FIXATE

Space Face

Cauldron contents of a toy chest:
popping candy of bodies mismatched,
upturned wheels, half-built worlds,
abandoned.

Gargling belly of fusspot picnics,
cross-eyed saucers cla ering under their gaga cups.
So lonely the aliens talk,
trying to convince me I am
not alone,
I want to believe, be
~~Alone~~. ~~—em~~. Somebody.

Sequinned silhoue es catch in the tangle of
friction-burnt knees
ski ering across a trampoline,
unsafe. Mental bouncing,
Pluto breaks. Constellations like you read about.
Is this Saturn's last return?

Tweaking the antennae of a grainy VHS transmission,
I just want to watch *Ghostbusters* 2, 2, 2 –
clumsy reel skips, like determined feet on February sand.
  e harder I push forward, the deeper my toes are swallowed.

Age eight, I get premature neck zits.
Zombie-bolts studded along my jugular,
unidentified spying objects
on psychogenic skin:
        play it cool,
        listen in, them,
        it's just God in grey flesh and an agent orange frock.

what u wearing?

do you want me to spill it
tell you that my face is masked in an adulthood I can't scrape
that I have an eternal weariness
worn as my mother's quiet
but unshakeable resolve
flaws that stand at a   ention because told so
beneath an unevenly bu   oned Snoopy vest
while my elbows freeze from being witnessed
with *#nomakeup*, but not in the glamorous way
insecurities pleated to half their size and with darts
that detumesce when I don't iron them smartly away
and zips that burst like an overboiled Hungarian
cheese kransky in an eruption of dull, dull innards
or shall I just admit I'm wearing trackpants
that look like Windows 98?

Dry-retching Into a Psych Ward Toilet Bowl (Christmas 2021)

How public – like a frog – Emily Dickinson

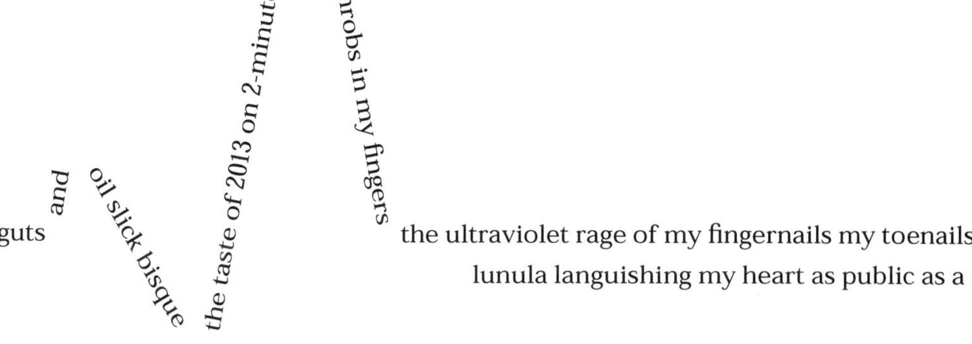
guts
and
oil slick bisque
the taste of 2013 on 2-minute noodles
sadness throbs in my fingers
the ultraviolet rage of my fingernails my toenails my
lunula languishing my heart as public as a frog

Days Madness Holds Me

I
evaporate
on
a
tongue
of
morning
stale
and
sleep-stained
wringing
my
veins
out
all
slop
and
sadness
something
snaps
dendrites
to
dander
goosebumps
custard
heart
ache
my
playground
days
wave-crash
into
daylight's
destiny
the
banana
peel
high
glitching
lavender
lechery
brain
sandy
with
salt
and
sage
awakening
suicide
a
chipped
shell
scabbing
to
pearl
by
milk
metaphor
and
madness

through
a
makeshi
midnight
eclipse
pixelating
its
catastrophe
from
delusion
pickling
sunset
and
vinegar
no
love
lost
but
something
found
in
moon-burnt
mumbling
goose
within
heart
break
is
stronger
holds

horizons
wobble
comfort
keeps
edges
fact
fiction
collapse
fear
delights
syrup
swamps
sugared
villains
sweat
laden
le overs
honeyed
something
poem
taxidermy
sky-sick
bumbling
teeth
maelstrom
by
mayhem
nothing
everything
me

Acne

I am picking pimples on public transport. Scab, scab, scab. e smell of mixed cologne is aggressively strong, each scent fighting for atmospheric dominance, trying to coax a sneeze any way they can. I won't give any of them the satisfaction. I know it's gross to peel away my flesh in public. People don't like that. Mutilate yourself in private. We don't want your fresh blood. Come back with a dignified scar. Talk to me when it calluses. Don't show your face until it scab, scab, scabs.

Acne is when you reach out to smooth a panic a ack like a crinkly dollar exchanged for a chocolate kiss, and I kick you wildly and run for the river's edge.

I am squeezing cysts in the city. Troy calls me Scaz, and I never remember why. Scaz, scaz, scaz. I am a tiny li le snail, and the cologne-stenched are waiting for me to die so their rough-n-tough hermit crabs can build a McMansion from my body, or a bubble of billionaires oozing from the craters in my face. But Troy says I'm hard too, rogue like an elephant you can't befriend, but a baby one, maybe. Do you ever look at a straight boy and wonder what kind of edgy bollocks he's spouting on Reddit, because you just know it's something?

It's a fun distraction from their leering – the kind where they're thinking about all the reasons they don't want to fuck you, and you are sick with banality from the expectation that you're supposed to care.

Acne is the blotched mystery of a filthy bathroom floor when you drill the door down and I shriek at you to let me die. I'm sixteen and I can't see straight enough to realise you're trying to help. It's not your fault. It's not mine either.

I am bursting blackheads under bridges. Healing leaves its tell-tale mark. Scar, scar, scar. It's unprofessional to go to a job interview without makeup, I learned. I ask if it's unprofessional to have skin and they think I'm making fun of them. It's a serious question. I want a serious answer.

But more so, I just want one thing for myself. I just want skin. Bad skin. And for that to be okay. I know I'm less like a social bu erfly and more like a well-intended moth. Yeah, you think I'm gross. But I'm here. I'm trying. I'm ready to be absorbed into your violently fluorescent universe. I'm also not sorry that I am just a moth.

Acne is when I let myself live. Alive with acne. Always with acne. But still, alive.

Perseverate

sever/e the spinning wheel as it s/tick/s fight the p/urge phineas disen/gage me throw the ice bucket of quix/neur/amni/otic milk of human kinda/ness s/pill soy sauce on the grim reaper rely too hard on the imagined ma/car/ena a snail is forever and so is—

(MAL)ADAPT

Funhouse

gumnut assorteds for supper
                              again
dry dust snorted   with weak earl grey
          before 8pm doses   when they   find   me
in a courtyard of sti   chairs and hazy   e dge s
                    made   h a z i e r
while I make   c r a z i e r ¿

I hoard sprinkles   secret colours in my ice cream
loud walls of chipped beige
                                             gnawed binge
                 by chipped teeth
they take me out   an a   ernoon on a co   on candy Ferris wheel
amusement park tragedy   of a dying child’s wish
we’re having fun   you must have fun
                                        I think so   your duty to have fun
----
                    it may as well   live inside
                                                  my   skin
          like every tiny dust mite
               that fucks and fights for survival

in pores   scrubbed   raw but never

unfilthy

until I cave   and exfoliate   with the dirts

feeding   slugs and symptoms

W o v e n

into neuroses

☒ *Try some b r e a t h i n g exercises*

☑ *Try instead*

screeching for benzodiazepines

soothing   ocean sounds like a

calculation of parrots

on linen shoulders

we describe ourselves as   seasons

Mary is the midsummer

her voice dry with the heritage and heartbreak

of a family who will never visit

I ramble about   crunchy leaves, vomit and screams

but she says   *No matter who we are today*

We all become   the

Fall

---

some things we just can't change
the weight of vulnerability   an ache of a Dr Pepper can on teeth
the bruising of blood pressure   an accidental Rorschach
the *splash*
sh of a zealous urine sample a frenzy of muppet arms
sh
all of the emotions today
just le 'em on the dinner tray

---

as a dog I must eat
my own vomit curled into
the intimacy of its echo
a synced period
cyclical as soy sauce pisces
and silica packets
straitmen threatening the jacket
they once said *growing pains*
as if the next ones weren't sharper yet
or duller than ever
or better off bed

Funhouse (~~Relapse~~ Reprise)

Here's where we're at: A nurse compliments me on my very interesting file, and I celebrate a pyrrhic victory against myself. I cut out a picture of a flea mechanic in art therapy. An older woman looks at it from over my shoulder and says, 'that's so you'. We've never met before, but somehow, she's right.

I'm back at the beginning.   ad nauseam. add nausea.
Shrink me
papercuts on a phantom limb // sandpaper serifs \\ no sharps
between the
too tired to give this beauty anymore
lines of a poem.
too clumsy to make it ~~memorable~~ meme-able.

But anyway, how was breakfast? [ey speak like sou   é.]

Any thoughts of self-harm?

[collapsed]

I'm not suicidal, I'm just—

---

a googly-eyed rock in the community garden.
how do I grow here? I've lost splinters in this skin. I can only –
s   r
p   i   n   l   the grains of salt
k   onto each of these wounds
e   and wastelands

The Last 37.5mg longitudinal collage of my diary

37.5

honeymoon of a headache
in this PG-13 skull of spacetime
the hairline ri between work and
working on it
really, I am.
am I?
I know it doesn't seem like it.
does it?
... can I swear here?

31.25

trying to fix things with the same futility
asking Siri for help when she just Googles like a common mortal.
how to stop being a dykey nightmare?
a dyke-mare?
[nay, that sounds like a lesbian horse.]
I FOUND THIS ON THE WEB FOR 'HOW
TOSTOPBEINGADAIKONNIGHTMARE'.
so, thanks for the radish salad recipes and air-con manuals.

25

on the train.
stewing in my own juices. like an angry bolognese.
had to buy fruit tingles so I wouldn't eat the dog's medicine.
[also ate a crayon.]

18.75

- the psychic who called me a stale marshmallow
- the bird that ate the elastic from my clotheslined underwear
- the cup-o-noodles trying to connect with me on Facebook
- the middle school mixtape of 'Hero' by Enrique, on repeat
- the brain zapz and psyche scraps

12.5

sleep sand on the rim of my margarita
melatonin metallic in my brain-folds
you only fall asleep from pretending you already are,
so I try this for everything else too.
fake it until you make it, a er all, and I can make dreams
where Healthy Harold emerges from my teeth and says,

I couldn't have saved you.

6.25

as I turn out of the driveway
I've never worried about leaving the stove on and starting a fire
but what if I le the vibrator gently buzzing in my nightstand
hornet's nest of horniness
stirring us into *terremoto*
surrendering to that wasp

motherfucker, there, I said it.

0.0

well,
I just called myself a *minestrone pony*
in the workplace

I guess I've reached lucidity now. I give it a 7 out of 10.

Marsha Loves an Acronym

fanDango pink pop-psych scum-bucket
thrEe parts mad and three hats madder
I am A hat but I am not your wife
the paRiah of group therapy
Mercurial and milk-sopped
holding rAge like heartburn
iNcalmo dialectics

fruitbody of my fragile Psyche
gaslight gate-boss girL-keep
I create a kErfu   e
barbed glAss nerve endings
burniShed ... and so on
edges bleEd into an outpatient ether

Insurance glitches
what is a Mood anyway?
traiPsing papertrail histories
reliving the gnaRled guts of a girlhood
quixOtic catacombs
holding un-Velvety mornings
buzzcut back to thE skin of my teeth

Freak Fruit

yes. I am struggling.

but of course, it isn't always easy
to be a weirdly disfigured lemon
trying to grow
around branches of bullshit
or the ligature of a tyre swing
knowing that you'll only ever sum to
looking vaguely like genitalia
but not being nearly as sweet.

you sourcunt.

Quiet Hands collage from medication instructions

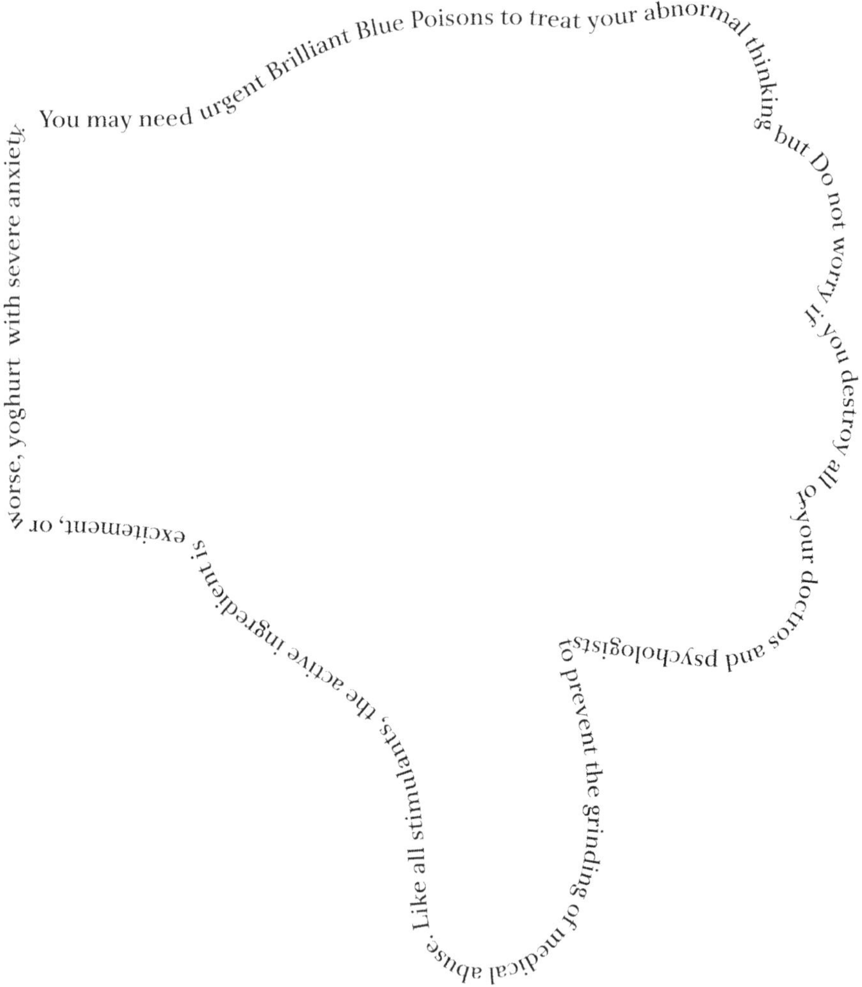

INTERACT

Fidget Spinster for Amelia Newman

Can you hear me? Wait – you're on mute!
Uh huh! Okay, I've got you now! It's me!
...
Yep, it's Velma's knobby knees,
the Grinch's gay mothers,
Elmo's favourite ice cream flavour – pistachio –
music that plays when Fiona turns from Princess to Princess Ogre.
...
Would you want carrots from my fanny pack? Probably not, huh?
My social script says not to ask people this, but if you could have
anything other than skin encasing your body, what would it be?
...
Juicy, juicy verbs. Bamboozle. Canoodle. Skedaddle.
...

REPLY **STOP** TO UNSUBSCRIBE.

...
Sorry for leaving so abruptly. I'm terrified of UTIs.
...
Is it possible to be a *Sharknado*, yet still boring?
It says a lot that the *Sims* universe doesn't allow for hate-fucking.
Not wi y enough for cool-girl poetry, not so   enough for subtlety.
...
Why isn't there a homunculus with a giant clit? I want to see an
uncensored sensory homunculus with a supermassive bell end,
out-of-this-world genitals.
...

STOP

...
Even in those spaces, I'm defined by an imagined proximity to
men. Like, call me a dyke, not a fag hag. We can't all be the kind of
gay that fits comfortably within a Kmart catalogue.
...

e oh-so subversive existence of cowering indoors and eating biscuits. Alone, as usual.

...

It's like I only exist within my own head. Indivisible zero ... that's a thing, right?

No, don't answer.

We can only fold in on ourselves so many times, I've heard.

at's real math.

...

You can't count on sunset that close to the arctic.

e heart itself isn't even heart-shaped.

...

Sometimes you have to sit in it, ripe and clinging like ... a soiled diaper. What's my GP gonna do? Tell me to drink water and stop being a bitch? Because I refuse to do either.

...

I keep crying over *Masterchef*. I love you like XO sauce. I just can't respond to your texts.

...

But, which did you wear best?

e loneliness or the sweater vest?

...

STOP

...

My list was unhelpful today:

Party toys that you can flick at people and leave marks on the wall that your dad banned from the house.

Pu y squished into carpet fibres.

Pizza le out long, gummy with no-thank-yous.

Papier-mâché, half-eaten.

Plain old grief.

...

All the sticky things.

...

Like licking your own uvula—no, *uvula.*

...

Like a well-used dildo, shoved into the drawer when their real friends come over.

...

Like a waterbed, wet, dreamy, and forge able. I guess we keep these childhoods somewhere, isotopic in our bones.

...

STOP

...

Gimme one hour of scream time.

Lazy Eyed

Brain skewed –

Snooker stripes in the
overgrown understory, untold –

Once-upon-a-times,
when I bargain-hunted down this rabbit hole too.

Haloed ligatures
against magic-eight

fated anomalies,
happening within and without

Me.
Astroturf asphyxia of lost cues.

Hold a mirror to my head,
with stigmata fingertips

racking the billiards –

A Voice that Angers Men on Public Transport

I thought I was
pre-supposed to be
the one with all that fucking
social impairment.

trying to hold
this crud in my throat
an act of amphibian alchemy
spi ing out galumphs
from la-di-da-di-das.
the echolalia of lily lily-livers.

[INSPECTOR] I wish that I could exist out here

and not end up
crying on a freeway
in a constant state of leaky lobotomy
each time an unknown man farts
an opinion
scrambling my synapses
to snot.

shame is a scab
of peanut bu er mucus
anchored to my gag reflex.
I can't breathe through it
but I can't swallow it either.
so, I hock it up to the clouds
until they finally send me rain.

I know I can only be phlegmatic
if I twist its definition
to simply mean
full of phlegm and fluids.
is this all *psycho-smegmatic*?
sometimes I get so flustered
that every word
starts to sound like
those hocus-pocus
euphemisms
Oprah invents to avoid saying the word vagina.

[INSPECTOR] Vagina.

feed me faux pas forgiveness
in sepia tones
like old-timey photographs that scream *aesthetic*
and croak *bubonic*.
I guess I like things that I can chew into soggy ammunition
because I may be an easy target
but you're not the one with the spitball.

Bazaaro World for Bertha

It's about as early as it gets on Sunday. e regulars are already set up, while the rookies are barely unpacking their stalls. One woman's passion appears to be fashioning lamps out of coca cola bo les. A wishbone necklace sits out of place on the table, a tu of rancid meat le un-scraped from its edge. is man likes birdseed – lots of birdseed – and tchotchkes that simp for patriotism. My dog eats doughnuts from the worn-down showgrounds. Yum. She licks a woman's leg idly: thanks for dropping your pastry. e woman veers away from me with contempt, yuck, as if I snagged the most a ractive Sydney 2000 Olympics memorabilia from under her nose. I hop along, flea-like.

I accidentally make eye contact with someone's pog collection, so naturally, they hard-sell to me for the next half hour. at's fair. A person peddles *Finding Nemo* on video – it's only fi y cents. Sold. Who doesn't still have a functioning VCR for the discounted tears of a clownfish? I can buy ten seasons of *Seinfeld*, even though only nine were made. I'm curious, but I opt against it. I don't need to see Jerry's future, but I wish Elaine the best.

ere's a pavilion that smells like parent-mandated sporting commitments. A stained man sells a ba ery-powered dog. He charges extra for ba eries that make it yap. A makeshi stall within the boot of a car sells second-hand fingernails and celebrity skintags. A posh head tszujs a $20 sign upon a rack of her old clothes. She's new to the circuit. Very new. I ask if I can buy her shoulder-padded vest for two dollars, and she shoos me away.

I show my dog a stu ed gira e: *whaddya think?* She sni s an approval. It only costs a dollar, but the seller snatches it away when she sees I don't intend it for a human child. Vendors get defensive about their possessions, even ones they don't want. I understand. A rusty deck chair is surrounded by po ed plants. Baby tears are too dry to weep. Some basil is labelled parsley, and I don't have the heart to tell the ba ered savs these home truths. I think of taking everything home and treating it like parsley. I'm tired. Fog ascends. Here, there are also dirts. Free of charge, trusty dirts.

From the ground, a ray of sunlight photographs young people with Polaroids and gold coins. From caravans to carnivals, we damp creatures must retreat. Until next week.

i ain't reading all that / i'm happy for you tho / or sorry that happened

She owed us so many poems – Keaton Pa i's AI-bot-inspired obituary

What if I don't have any poems le in me? Don't talk to me until I've had my cosmic comeuppance. It doesn't ma er what happened to me in private; people will only ever remember that I was publicly insane. I used to love honey and fear drugs. Now I'm all drugs and bees, no sweetness. Perhaps I'm only human if you believe in me hard enough, if I'm sensible and sympathetic and ever so good. Enchanted by another snail, I weave desire paths through my own muck. Would I still make an iconic lollipop lady? Something, something, something fugue. In the emergency department, we are a series of questions without an appropriate checkbox. e waiting room full of false rainbows and unknown variables. My coming out story is the ballad of Earring Magic Ken. I don't want to perform wellness, but I don't want to perform sickness either. In your dreams, my mouth is Velcro, spilling scratchy secrets. In mine, my fears crumble to salt and I eat them on French fries. You untie my shoes for me when I'm too tired to put myself to bed. I don't notice until the next morning, when I'm moulding my feet back into shape. In the (psycho)tropics, nine out of ten GPs are frothing to shame my body for how it responds to antipsychotics. I recover from the eating disorder, and they breathe a sigh a relief that I am fodder for their fatphobia once more. I am diagnosed as a character from *Chicken Run*. I am both the nerd and the di in *Chicken Run*. I am the utopic lesbian aspirations of *Chicken Run*. e world is full of scheming plasticine rats, just like *Chicken Run*. I'm in love with the shape of *Chicken Run*. What does it mean when you get the Tuesday Suicides every day? I masturbate: is that a li le suicide? I make a nest from my own hair because I don't trust anyone else's. I am a private menace, disturbing my own peace. All I want is to dilly dally. Too much dilly, not enough dally. Or vice versa. A dilly dally dilemma. I wish I could stifle the sound of my chaos into the tune of *The L*

Word theme song. A di erent song plays. It's the music from reality TV dating shows that indicates a contestant is an u er clown. I don't want to kill a fly for buzzing. I don't want to destroy something simply because it's annoying. January melts and mumbles. Sorry for se ing o your uncanny valley detector. Does this valley have a campground?

My dad tells me of when his family home burned down around him, but he refused to leave until someone made him a ketchup sandwich.

It's this, more than the shape of our elbows, that convinces me of genetics. I'm one minor inconvenience away from becoming a cartoon supervillain. I name my absent children a er the noises in the a ic, and all words lose their meaning. ey call it semantic satiation. I fill in the blanks with *lorem ipsum*. Under this roof, we go o impulse. I'm addicted to competition shows where the judges cry a lot. I watch Insta videos of some guy eating porridge while covered in rodents. Frisson itches. You go away for a week, and I forget to nurture the parts of myself that make me a person. I let a spider claim the kitchen. e dog claims the bedroom, the cat claims my skin. I've never once felt refreshed in my life. Standing around like a person emoji, I fixate on hyperdontia. Hyperdontia wish your girlfriend had teeth like me. I want to be angry so badly, a pre-emptively clenched fist. My fursona is the dust monster from *Round the Twist*. It's easier to live in corners. Each cluster of breath tastes like a mistake, a sunflower smoke. Are these pareidolic faces mad at me? I am Zac Efron's pond reflection in the 'Bet On It' number in *High School Musical 2* – a shi ily edited facsimile of a star. All lesbians are jellicles, but craving oat milk instead of rebirth. At a social function, I tell someone's grandpa that I'm a tooth-eating dentist to conceal my identity as a tooth-wearing poet. Is it so wrong to write? Less of a river, more of a sludge-covered rock jammed in its craw. My assailant is now someone's husband; I'm wed only to my willpower. He's the apple of her eye, but he squirms at my core, a toxic gut full of worms, soured. I'm the bridegroom of sweet revenge, cold revenge, of revenge for the ragamu n, rascal, rapscallion, rat bastard. ere's a bunion bioluminescent on the cusp of my life. I'm ripping out the tags and cosplaying in your old clothes. In queer company, and only here, I'm suddenly feminine. I was always the boy in the playground, the honorary husband, frog, or piece of furniture, if I was ever permi ed to play at all. I'm a disaster of a girl, but I refuse to be anything else. Mrs. Jingles died today. I spent my first day of school playing hide-and-seek, with no one coming to find me. I don't own an accurately functioning clock, not even the *Shrek* one. Time skips. I step out of this poem for a few days. I'm more flexible than people think, contorting into yoga poses, packing myself up like a saggy old ma ress, drenched in campfire beans. ere's an apricity to my burnout on a crisp morning, curling my singed edges. If life were an urban legend, I'd be a mere gerbil and the world would be Richard Gere's bu . All my targeted ads describe themselves as 'bu erso ', and I develop a Pavlovian response to my non-dairy margarine alternative spread. I doom-scroll too hard, entering a dimension where my least favourite person lip-synchs my least favourite song (and they're not even a drag queen). At dawn, I walk past all the rich houses in a neighbouring suburb, their silence like a status symbol.

I pick my wedgie as I pass the fanciest mansion. I am the Garfield of this very moment. Every alien abduction story is weirdly horny; I just want extra-terrestrial kinship.

I rejuvenate my line readings, soap-scummed and palms pruning. We load up on discount vegetables at NQR, but you're the only one who envisions what they can become. Alone, I pu up spores. I'm that person buying the trendy flavours of classic products – Oreos, crisps. Is it my fault there's Vegemite everything? e world's greatest poem is whatever is going through my dog's mind when she nibbles on my fingernail. I can't compete with that, but why are we always competing? Maybe this is enough, whatever it is. Scream-happy in a Spotlight store, I stifle conspiracy theories about their ugly, bland fabrics. I morph into a nightmare femme on the floor of a Bunnings, bleeding gli er glue. I saw a turtle today, but there were already two people with nose rings taking pictures of it, and I didn't want to make it three of us. A villain, or a cat from the *Cats* musical, says 'I am'. A hero, or a poet, says 'I want'. But I am what I want, and I want to be a poetic cat. e teddy bear on the side of the road destroys me with a siren song. Each day is an heirloom fruit. I never learnt to play chess. I fill my time with rodent funerals, spacing out beneath an uninvited daytime moon. I lived with someone for four years without ever knowing the scrawl of her handwriting. I want to plant enough trees to o set my existence. is sounds like shit when Siri reads it. Does it sound any be er in my voice? In your head? Why must I always wait to be emboldened, struck by lightning, before I can say a word? Poetry is so fucking embarrassing.

Mindblind

It is the cut inside your cheek –
felt every second
with world – none the wiser,
as teeth contort back to crooked,
crooked comfort.

It is a dog ear, inside-out,
a seashell of loudness and lyme,
or a feeling of wrongness,
back-to-front
and around-the-twist.

It is a 4am infomercial
for the rust of Rumpelstiltskin.

It is a slug in the sinuses,
a whi of words like milquetoast and quasar,
but only the promise of
an ill-timed sneeze.

It is the 52-megaher whale.

It is the disharmony
of canned yucks in 90s sitcoms –
the trailing giggle as Ross sports a season-long boner,
and the too-hard gu aw as Raymond hates his family,
every. insipid. episode.

It is a honeycomb full of ants,
and a bucket of brain sand
castled into moats and magic eyes.

It is being your pet project.
Hannah Gadsby now sells rocks.

It is a Milo tin
in the apocalypse.
Comforting, but for whom?

It is the shit
le un-smeared.

I Can't Stop Thinking About Jake Gyllenhaal's Fuck the Patriarchy Keychain

I sob harder for my starving Neopets
than I can for my own sex
assault. I censor the word:
~~rope~~
~~ripe~~
~~rape~~.
I'm not a man writing about divorce or gumnuts,
which is to say my poetry is cook smart.
I know now I was never
deranged,
only degraded to the point where I cannot
metabolise my own history.
Stone fruit in my gall bladder, my kidneys: ectoplasmic.
I give birth to stone children, freak fruit
that tear me open all over again.
Nobody tells you that you'll piss yourself,
then become unable to piss.
Nobody tells you that you'll scab over,
crusty eyes and keloid scars.
Nobody tells you that you'll fill your house
with packing tape, FRAGILE only.
Nobody tells you that the details will emerge
like a magician's mouth scarf, a soggy and endless pappardelle.
Nobody tells you that your pussy will go into bankruptcy,
maybe forever.
On LinkedIn, he dabbles in cyber activism:

BOYS
WILL BE
~~BOYS~~
HELD ACCOUNTABLE

a er Patricia Lockwood

I don't know my knees anymore,
never used them to dance.
I safety-pin the skerrick of a thought, surrogate emotion,
patching together something that may one day resemble fury.
A doctor dons gloves out of my secant of vision
and announces their sterility.
I ask, 'Do you want to talk about it?'
It's always the teeth,
clumsily wielded,
blunt instruments fighting sharp objects.
Sick bay betrayals, folding in on myself
an impossible number of times,
moment and memory sauté. Pink pepper, anyone?
I dare to be a hag, zit-dappled, trimming my pubes to 'All Star'.
Bewitched milk lines souring, trailing in the ultraviolet.
My psychiatrist draws my consciousness
and it looks like a bu hole.
Shit's always coming into here, into your consciousness, he says.
Shit's always coming out of there too, by the looks of it,
the pucker responds.
My dog desecrates the shallow grave of a magpie
and, caked with dirt and tears,
I learn that I am full of salt corpses
and beast prints. e shadow of a wing
in a venus fly trap's undiscerning gut.
Wild blackberries and a kissyface of cobwebs,
Quicksilver, goosebumps, inescapable.
Nobody tells you its tedium,
how you wake up the next day and keep upright.
Nobody tells you that it sits beneath your skin,
mycelia aching to mushroom, toxically, tragically edible.
Nobody says a fuckin' word.

BEHAVE

James Joyce's Fart Fetish

Shroom dust in a shisha pipe,
bubbles in the dregs of your milkshake
burning a hole in my carpet.
School of Rock with a scabby angel,
rusty but un-rustic: too poor to tickle a hipster's ding-a-ling.
Do you need another? I'll take one anyway.
(Is this treating myself?)
Jack Black is raving and retching
out of the television like the li le girl from *The Ring*.
You know that's Lilo, right?
She never wants it to rain because her parents died there.
...
It's true, Mozart loved ge ing his ass eaten.
No, I swear! I'll look it up right now!
See? – Bu holes have taste-holes.
Huh? Tastebuds, tastebuds.
Like a Portrait of the Fartist as a Young –
Stop, I'm not ready. I'm young.
I'm too young.
...
Concept: a Fleshlight in a boot, call it 'Puss In'.
All this innovation, and for what?
A capricious fizzle as I'm sogged up and dredged out,
trying to wash my hair like a
commercial mirage selling an over-lit dream.
Give me the towel. Get out.
I might be vulgar, but I don't want this.
...

Hey, when can we catch up?
Are you free?
...
Don't fucking slip me the tongue and blame it on Freud.
I may be stoned, but I still hate this.
...
Oh, you want money for those drugs
from like, a year ago?
I o ered at the time.
Huh? I'm a pariah or a parasite, but I can't be both.
...
Sure, you're hung
like a ird Reich zeppelin
with sexual charisma like garbanzo beans
or like you're the Man from Cranbourne
ge ing his moment on *A Current Affair*.
...
I just want to go home, or anywhere else,
even Cranbourne.
Maybe.

God Wants You to Come!

collage from pornography and religious magazines

BE BAPTISED. FAPWORTHY for the Lord.
He says, 'I WILL COME in a warm apple pie like
SEXodus Exodus'
mooing MEAT FOR Magic
Goose bumps and Gallic BLUMPKINS

FORSAKE the patriarch's TABOO TONGUE
JIZZNESS CAREER of the Holy Spirit
Isn't it wonderful to lobotomise Cupid
and abort e cream of His Euro-dorks?

Pray for cray cray! Upon the altar in your bosom
We call on the name of the FROGGY fucktress
who maketh a Psalm or a cup of rum,
naughty niceties in her blood garden.

THANK WANK that our God is a
Kleenex-wasting kill-joy.
Let heaven HANDJIVE!
as Hell LOLs!

Need a mint? One of those li le ones in tins from Coles?

Aspic

Treat my mind like a set dessert. Put it in a brain-shaped container, even though I prefer the little dinosaurs. Leave it in the fridge until it coagulates into the desired form. It may keep up the act. It looks ready to stand alone, to be flipped outwards to jiggle proudly on a plate, molecularly sound. But it splats heavy and cumbersome, too liquid inside. In freedom, it slops into the same puddle it always was, its few congealed nuggets the flotsam of a failed experiment. Let me stay runny.

Dreams that My Diary Unfortunately Remembers

– I laughed so hard that my jaw unhinged and I couldn't pop it back in place. I was repurposed as one of those clown heads in the carnival game where you shove things down their gullet to win a prize. I was rigged. I could never let anyone win, as much as I wanted.

– I split my tongue, split it again, and again, until it was like linguini strands. And, then, when I actually ate pasta, it was a frightening and confusing experience. I specifically remember the moment I split myself one too many times and I lost the ability to control each tongue strand independently. Prehensile pasta.

Baked ziti, Tony?

– Condoms were sold as ravioli with a choking-hazard.

– We turned a sharp corner and there were explosions in front of us shaped like animal heads crying tears of blood. It felt as horrifying as if they were real heads. We went through a door to the next room, and the Queens of the Stone Age were there, playing with cockatoo skeletons.

Somehow, I knew my terror was their doing.

– It was my funeral. You gave the eulogy: *She really put the bitch in obituary.*

– I got one of those Barbies that spins and flies like a fairy, but when I went to pick it up a er its first flight, it turned out to actually be a flying fox. I sat at my desk and started crying, and I realised in front of me was omas Nagel's philosophical paper 'What Is It Like to Be a Bat?', and then I knew what it was like to be both bat and Barbie.

####### – Everyone asked me for relationship advice, so I just kept aggressively whispering, 'make them do the Macarena.'

######## – On death row, my last meal request was 'Jennifer Aniston's name'.

Milk Teeth

firsts.

it hurts the moment we breathe
we su   er
as we episiotomy into existence
before all else
with
no teen movie summer fling
no tragic backstory
to teach us
how
delicate heartstrings sever
by the yelp of
a dog
its paw accidentally trodden on
the first and only
crying missile
of a glass cannon
that echoes somewhere,
in forever.

befores.

a contortionist of time and space
agonises the acrobatics of
                    pancreatitis and family violence
    twisting her gut
until, soon,
        she bruises the Earth right back, at last.

nexts.

the desert is undanceable
maybe this is just
how deserts are
    eroding into their own dunes
    with supervised lunchtimes
        in case of violence, vomit
and the two weeks it took before
forcibly, foreseeably
    your bare feet singed
    to a blister turned all singsong-like and bully-boiling
        psycho dyko
        you're a crazy bitch
        a stone's throw from here,
        you'd be stoned to death.
                                        sure, maybe.
                                        we can only hope.

afters.

my ingénue is dead
I know it
I shed
words,
naturally as skin cells,
and she flakes away like
the chrysalis of a sunburn
infinitesimally creepy
the dustsceawung
of the fact that I am here
my voice no longer ... no longer something
I look him in the eye, even
my brow more creased
than his suit has ever been
my ingénue, dead, impatient
but still,
I smile for her
when I welcome the fate
that comes with the words
go fuck yourself.

evers.

to talk in circles would route me
to where I began
but
in spirals
a single line almost never
reaches
back at itself like an asp
to say
how devastating it is to hear
you have promise
knowing that promises
inherently
will become fulfilled
but humans
are, or
more o en,
not.

COMMUNICATE

Birth-controlled Dyke

Bu er me up
with hormone heresy
Bu er me up, bu er-fuck
so I don't get
ba ered
in the street
consequences evaporate
like dormant
funnel-webs in crumpets
doubling bubbling
toilet troubles
two-minute eternity in a piss-fingered cubicle
where our futures sweat with ... well, okay, maybe it's ghee?

Bu er me up
with a bulletproof body
Bu er me up, bu er-cuck
so I don't have to beg when they

S p r e a d m e
for break fast
threatening incontinence
and plumbing a pipe dream
just let me avoid the medical bill and anksgiving Bu erball
of predators on parole
but you still want your bread and bu - bu - bu er
from contraceptive camouflage
and
low-rent lesbians.

Bu er   me   up
with barrenness
Baste me
without excuses
that still m
e
l
t in your gob
bu ering
splu   t   te   r   ing
u ering
that I am
paranoid by delusion   turned destiny
hysterical for a hysterectomy
tongue-tied or tubular
lather us   smother us

mother!
un-mother us.
Drape your witch tits in cabbage to lactate, leaky, lucked out.

Or, just bu er me up,
Bu ercuppy.

Infodump

Is it sacrilegious to masturbate on Christmas? Or to eat pussy on Good Friday? My sanities lapse. A skeleton dipped in anxiety holds a dinosaur in its mouth, frog in its fleshless throat. Goose-teeth garro e. An ecosystem aches. Fruit accumulates in the room somehow. Unnerving as o -brand cartoon characters in a defunct fairground; intrusive as imperfect silence; haunting as love le ers inscribed in second-hand books. Care is a mycology. It's made of grrl* germs and your mother's gardening Crocs. I unlocked a formative memory: my grandmother forge ing my existence, si ing on me, failing to perceive my egg of a body. Crackling bones, milky and resilient. I don't have thoughts anymore, and I can't remember the last time that I did. I don't have bones anymore. I spy resting blur face, a captcha-confused entity. I wish I could autocorrect 'human cruelty' for 'hummus' in its every instance. Or make smiles out of similes. is chaos is so far from so , the kind that sits deep and panging like mushroom sprouts from molar grooves. ese ungentle ways of being. Tried outside today, where salt slugs fizzle in confe ied sunlight; where possums sizzle nightly on the powerline; where I dizzy dizzy dizzy on despair, delicately scraping a fla ened bird carcass o the street. Bury it beneath an accidental bloom, tangled life from the other side of the fence.

Æsj æsj!

Chaos crystallises as an ejaculate of concrete hitching a ride in the sole of my shoe – my sock, even – searching for sanity.

Call it a crisis. Or a meat-lovers pizza.

Insubordinate collage from formal warnings and disciplinary le ers

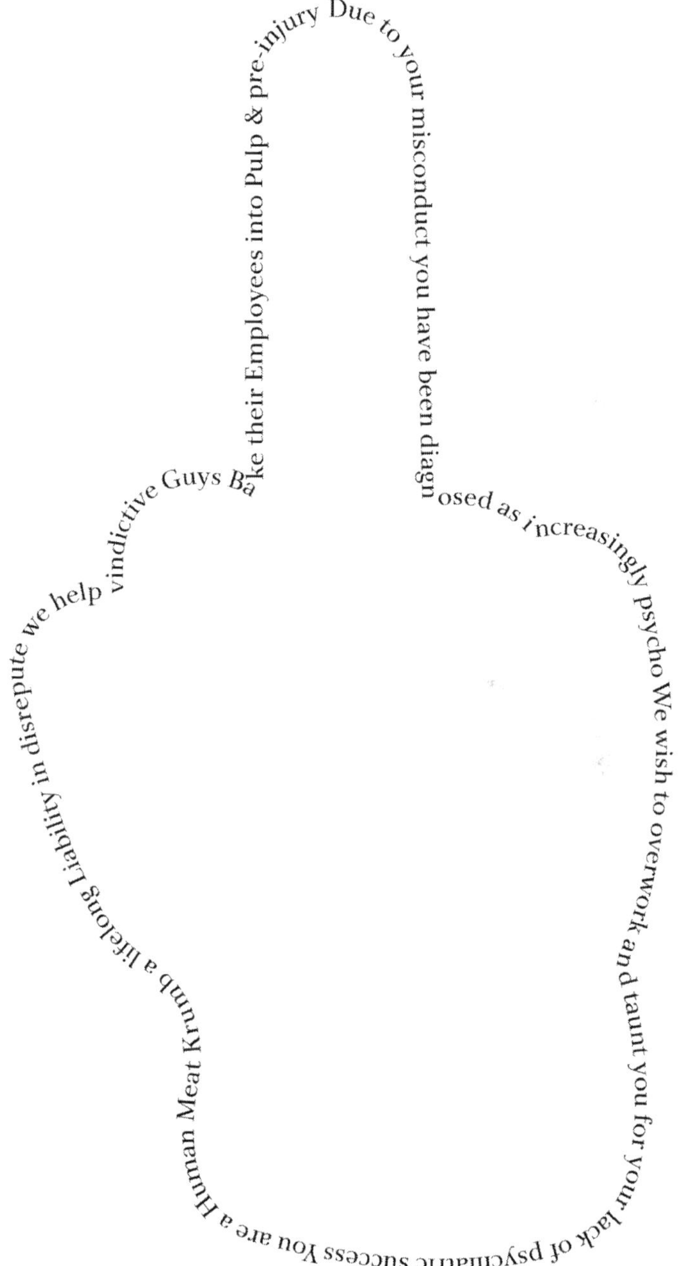

Girls Gone Wild   collage from a pornography magazine

1.
She felt A PANG DEEP inside
this time, moaning some sort of spell in Latin
It's a bloody RIOT to have skewered his arse on a metal rod
Is it that painful?
It doesn't ma er.

2.
Cenosillicaphobia is the fear of HUSBAND MATERIAL!
Twelve inches of piss and shit
big, wrinkly arseholes – wife-beaters, stubbies, Southern
Cross ta s and a VB.
+ MORE MINDLESS KILLING MACHINES
are they not?

3.
NICE TO CRY OVER THEM, *cos they're, y'know*, EMPTY.
I want to freeze his penis
& put it in a vacuum cleaner.
Two Panadols and he'll be
shi ing his wetsuit,
BUT IT IS STRANGELY SOOTHING ...

4.
Divorced Barbie had enough of her hubby.
cranky psychos
fire up leaf-blowers at 6am and chuck dog shit over a back fence.
SEX; it's too boring.
I'll stick with my nana's advice: beware the dedicated pissheads,
Slap yourself hard and shake it o .
then, humanely terminate me?

5.

Let's EAVESDROP INTO TWO LESBIANS
Full of life-a rming beauty like
a hat made out of McDonald's fries.
Warning: May cause GAY in big le ers.
LET IT DRIP FROM YOUR MOUTH.
burn somewhere in hell,
BECAUSE IT'S WORTH IT.

6.

filled with A GLASS OF GAY!
SHE ain't scared to make you weep.
Seriously mate, hit the fart sack.
We know how to cope with any vaginal grit
know we all rock
like a champion homo
and I don't know any other way.

On Special

1.

Hold me like hospital hands,
squared-eyed and cubist in the cranium.
It all happens and happens and—
Sorry, I just need to do your obs for the night.
His talcum phlegm
chalks yesterday's sneeze,
chokes me
with a slap of latex.
Clip my supervised toenails.
Don't forget your socks.
Bare feet are dangerous,
but you're safe.
So safe here.

2.

No, I'm not o ended.
We can discuss it all:
– each pair of shoes I can't grow into,
– the toys I don't grow out of,
– these things I won't become.
I have no other choice.
No, no! I'm really not o ended!
...
Have no other choice.

3.

Cut your throat from the inside out.
Egg-shelled oesophagus,
soggy and perforated and perfect as you.

Let me build a nest from polio death like the bones of a treehouse
carried by its still-blossomed brother.
I've got a birdlike appetite, and by this I mean
I pick at carcasses and swoop your bleach-breathed children
until they're down the hatch and vomiting underpants.

4.
A snow cone upturned on the sidewalk,
I cannot reach inside until I melt.
Melt. I need help.
Bleeding blue raspberry
in Ramadan,
through the blacked-out windows
of Howl's Moving Casbah.
Seven types of sand, did you know? Does it ma   er?
I buy Frankenstein and fried rice
in the absence of all else.
Ten years of
howling into melted dust,
but what will come next –
its echo or an ending?

5.
Bodies of blisters, bowlegged,
so topical I rub them into broken skin.
My pieces are missing because I ate them in the womb.
A mother's bile regurgitated,
varicose veins in a venus trap,
genetic flaws: my only life to live.

And I'd eat you too.

ACKNOWLEDGEMENTS

anks to Kent MacCarter for his mentorship, friendship and ongoing commitment to my career. It is everything – u erly life-changing. And to Rae White for their generous introduction.

ank you to my university tutors, Joan Fleming and John Hawke. I never thought I'd be dainty enough for poetry: you showed me that I don't have to be and allowed me to be your thirstiest student (your words, not mine).

Some of these poems have appeared in *Antithesis Journal, Australian Poetry Journal, Best of Australian Poems 2023, Bramble Journal, Cordite Poetry Review, Five:2:One Magazine, Ramona Magazine, Scum Magazine, Slam Chop, SWAMP Magazine, The Victorian Writer, The Writing Place 2021* and *Whale Road Review*. My thanks to the editors. ank you to my mentors, Jennifer Harrison, Andy Jackson, Melody Paloma, Fiona Wright, Paul Yore and the organisations that supported me, including Arts Access Australia, Express Media, Midsumma, e Wheeler Centre and Writers Victoria.

To my friends, colleagues and anyone else who touched these poems at any point, thank you endlessly.

To Amelia Newman, my hear hrob, thank you for loving a poet: a creature both deeply sensitive and deeply annoying. For the nights I climbed over you to get to my computer and write stu down, for the times I became cagey when you asked about my poems, for the huge ways you support me with the most basic tasks, day in, day out. No one else sees it, but I do.

To Ki y and Kiwi, thank you for chasing me out of bed and forcing me to face each day.

Alex Creece is a writer, collage artist and average kook living on Wadawurrung land. She works as online editor for *Archer Magazine* and production editor for *Cordite Poetry Review*. She is also on the editorial commi ee for *Sunder Journal*. Creece has been awarded fellowships with Arts Access Australia, Midsumma Pathways, e Wheeler Centre and Writers Victoria. Her work has been shortlisted for the Born Writers Award, Geelong Writers Prize, Kat Muscat Fellowship, Next Chapter Scheme and the Lord Mayor's Creative Writing Award. ank you my teams at *Archer Magazine*, *Cordite Poetry Review* and *Sunder Journal*.